1°/96

Why We Left

I Remember
CHINA

Anita Ganeri

RAINTREE
STECK-VAUGHN
PUBLISHERS
The Steck-Vaughn Company

Austin, Texas

Published by Raintree Steck-Vaughn Publishers, an imprint of Steck-Vaughn Company

Editors: Sally Matthews, Jim Pipe, Carol Callahan
Designer: Peter Bennett
Cover Design: Joyce Spicer
Illustrator: Dave Burroughs
Photo Research: Brooks Krikler Research

Library of Congress Cataloging-in-Publication Data

Ganeri, Anita, 1961–
    I remember China / Anita Ganeri.
        p.   cm. — (Why we left)
    Includes index.
    ISBN 0-8114-5608-0
    1. China—Juvenile literature. I. Title.
    II. Series.
DS706.G36 1995
951.05—dc20
                              94-21852
                              CIP

Printed and bound in Belgium

1 2 3 4 5 6 7 8 9 0 PR 99 98 97 96 95 94

Contents

Introduction

Hello! My name is Sun Dan. I am from China. I was born in Beijing, the capital of China. You may know it as Peking. My family and I had to leave China. My parents did not agree with the strict rules and laws of the Communist government. If we had stayed in China, our lives would have been very difficult. We feel much safer and freer in the United States.

I still miss China and all my friends and relatives. Come with me and find out about China. I'll help you learn about its long history, its culture, and its people.

After 1949, it was very difficult for Chinese people to leave China. Tourists as well as Chinese living abroad could not easily visit China. More people are allowed in and out today. However, many Chinese prefer to live in the West. The United States and Canada are two of the countries in the West where many of us now live.

Welcome to China

China is in southeastern Asia. It is a huge country, the third largest in the world. Only Russia and Canada are larger. It's about the same size as all of Europe! China stretches from Tibet in the west to the East China Sea (part of the Pacific Ocean) in the east. It stretches from the Mongolian border in the north to the Vietnam border in the south. Apart from its long coastline, its land borders on 11 countries. China itself is divided into 22 provinces and five regions.

The official name for China is People's Republic of China. The ancient Chinese called their country "Zhongguo," meaning "Middle Kingdom," because it was the center of the world for them.

你好

One-fourth of the world's population speaks Chinese! Instead of letters joined to make words, we use symbols, called characters, which we learn by heart. Each one stands for an idea or a word. This is how we write "Hello" (left). When Chinese words are written in English, the letters *zh* are pronounced "j" as in "jeans," and the letter *q* is pronounced "ch" as in "chip."

RUSSIA

MONGOLIA

GOBI DESERT

GREAT WALL

TAKLAMAKAN
DESERT

CHINA

Beijing

Huang
Ho R.
(Yellow R.)

Grand
Canal

NORTH
KOREA

SOUTH
KOREA

TIBET

SICHUAN

Xi'an

Chang Jiang R
(Yangtze R.)

Shanghai

East China Sea

HIMALAYA MOUNTAINS

NEPAL

INDIA

BHUTAN

TAIWAN

BANGLADESH

MYANMAR
(Burma)

Guangzhou

Hong Kong

LAOS

Mekong R.

THAILAND

VIETNAM

South China Sea

CAMBODIA

MALAYSIA

Country and Climate

The land and climate of China are different from region to region. To the west lie the wild and windswept Tibetan-Qinghai plateau and the snow-capped Himalaya mountains. One of these mountains, Mount Everest, on the border of Nepal and Tibet, is the world's highest mountain. In northern China are the Gobi and Taklamakan deserts. They are hot during the day and freezing cold at night. Southern China is much warmer and wetter. It has a tropical climate. Most people live in the eastern part of China, along the banks of two great rivers. They are the Yangtze (Chang Jiang) and the Yellow River (Huang Ho). The land nearby is good for farming. But about two-thirds of China is too hilly or too dry to farm.

The giant panda is China's most famous animal. Pandas live in the bamboo forests of the Sichuan Mountains. They are now very rare, because so much of their natural habitat has been cleared for farmland.

An Ancient People

For over 3,000 years, China was ruled by powerful dynasties (royal families). The first emperor to unite China was Shih Huang-ti in 221 B.C. The emperor also ordered work to begin on the Great Wall (far right), to keep out northern invaders. When he died, he was buried with an army of thousands of life-sized terracotta (clay) soldiers (right). In 1974, these were discovered by accident in the city of Xi'an. Many other dynasties followed after that. At the beginning of the twentieth century, however, ordinary people fought back against the wealth and power of the emperors. The last emperor was overthrown in 1911. In 1912, China became a republic.

The ancient Chinese are famous for inventions. Gunpowder, silk, paper, and the magnetic compass are a few. Invented in tenth-century China, the abacus (left) is still used today.

8

Communist China

In 1949, Mao Zedong (Mao Tse-tung), the head of the Chinese Communist Party, became leader of the People's Republic of China. The Communists believed in a society where everyone was equal. All property was owned by the whole community, not by individuals. They took land from wealthy landowners and set up "collective" farms. There, groups of peasant farmers shared the land and the work. The Communists also tried to rebuild China's economy. There was a big price to pay.

In 1966, Mao launched the Cultural Revolution. For ten years China was ruled by terror and violence. (Left) Groups of young people, called Red Guards, beat up and killed anyone they suspected of criticizing Mao. Nobody felt safe, even if they had done nothing wrong. Many tried to leave or left China.

Mao Zedong was born in 1893 and died in 1976. He was the leader of China from 1949 to 1976. In many ways, he was a great leader and thinker who tried to improve the lives of the poor. However, he was also very ruthless. Millions of people suffered and died during this period. Many ancient buildings and priceless treasures were also destroyed. Despite this, he is still a person of importance in the development of China.

The People of China

More than 1,178,000,000 people live in China. That's over four times as many people as in the United States. My family and over 92 percent of the people are Han Chinese. Our ancestors have lived in China since ancient times. There are also 56 smaller, or minority, groups. Many of these people live on the Chinese borders and in remote parts of the country. They include the Zhuang people in the south, the Manchu in the north, the Hui, and the Tibetans. Many have kept their own language and traditions.

In the past, Chinese people had large families to help with the farming and housework. Children took care of their parents as they grew older. Now, the Communist government has strongly encouraged couples to have just one child, so families are much smaller.

In China, older people are greatly respected. Their views and advice are always taken seriously. However, many older people still work hard in the factories or in the fields. They would probably be retired if they lived in the United States.

Chinese families use a very precise set of names for relatives. Sons and daughters are numbered, so that, for instance, if you were talking to an uncle who is the second son of your grandparents, you would call him "number two uncle." However, the exact word you use for your relative depends on whether they are on your mother's or your father's side of the family.

Most families in the city live in apartments owned by their work unit. Compared with apartments and houses in the West, there is usually a lot less space for everybody. It can also get very crowded outside. Compare the Shanghai street scene above with that in London's Chinatown (right).

City Life

Less than a third of Chinese people live in towns or cities. Even so, China has some of the biggest and most crowded cities in the world. The capital city is Beijing. It is the largest city in China, by area. Shanghai, on the east coast, has the largest population. Over 12 million people live there, more people than in New York or London. Most city families live in apartments in tall buildings. There are usually only two rooms that are both bedrooms and living rooms. Some families share kitchens and bathrooms.

In the cities, people shop at street markets, small general stores, and big department stores run by the government. Some of them are called "Hundred Goods Stores." They sell many different things. Very few people have enough money to buy expensive items.

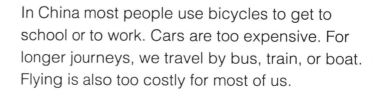

In China most people use bicycles to get to school or to work. Cars are too expensive. For longer journeys, we travel by bus, train, or boat. Flying is also too costly for most of us.

Rural Life

Two-thirds of Chinese people live in the country. Most work as farmers. The main crops are wheat in the north and rice in the south. Some farmers also grow millet, soybeans, cotton, fruit, vegetables, and tea, and raise pigs, ducks, and chickens. The farmland is owned by the government and rented out to families. Farmers must give part of what they grow to the government. They can sell the rest at market.

In Northern China, small farmhouses of mud or clay have thatched or tiled roofs. The farmhouses don't have running water or electricity. Water must be fetched daily from a well. Inside, there may be a raised brick bed, called a *kang*. This is heated like a stove. In winter, the whole family uses it for warmth.

Farmers have to work very hard to make a living. Most of the work is done by hand. Water buffalo are used for plowing the fields. There are some tractors. But they are too expensive for most farmers to buy.

School and Work

In China, we go to school from 7 A.M. until 6 P.M. six days a week. We start primary school at age six or seven (right). We learn Chinese and English, and study math, politics, crafts, and PE (physical education). Then we go to secondary school when we are about 12 years old. Some children leave school early to help their parents in the fields. Many students go on to study at the university. Others are given jobs by the government and start work.

Many people work in factories, making steel, textiles, bicycles, and machines. Factories are expected to look after their workers and provide them with houses, schools, and medical care. In China, both parents work.

Chinese doctors use both modern drugs and traditional treatments, such as acupuncture and herbal medicines. These are now becoming popular in the West, too.

Beliefs

Religious beliefs are not encouraged in China. They don't agree with many Communist ideas. In the past, though, religion played a more important part in people's lives. Some people follow the teachings of the philosopher, Confucius, who lived in the sixth century B.C. Taoism is another major religion. Its founder, Lao Zi, lived at the same time as Confucius. A third religion is Buddhism. It is still followed in Tibet, although many temples have been destroyed. There are also small groups of Muslims and Christians living in China.

Our most important celebration is the New Year festival. It falls between January 21 and February 19. We put up red paper decorations (for good luck), prepare lots of food, and exchange gifts.

In the Chinese calendar, each new year is named after one of 12 animals. The year of the rat is the first year, followed by the year of the ox.

Though many Chinese people are too poor to own refrigerators (above), we use other methods of preserving food, such as salting and drying (above left). Eating is a social occasion. We spend a long time eating and talking, especially when relatives are visiting.

Food and Clothes

There are Chinese restaurants all over the world. Most serve Cantonese-style food, which comes from Guangzhou (Canton) in southeast China. The ingredients used are often different from those used in China. However, there are lots of other styles of Chinese cooking. Some are hot and spicy. Others are sweet and sour. A typical meal consists of thin strips of vegetables, with pieces of meat cooked in a curved metal pan, called a wok. Most of our food is stir-fried (cooked very quickly in hot oil). We also eat noodles or rice.

Instead of plates, knives, and forks, we eat from small bowls using chopsticks. Duck is expensive, so we don't eat it very often. Tea is the most popular drink.

When the Communists came to power, people started wearing very plain and simple clothes. These blue or gray cotton jackets and pants were comfortable and practical for work. Many people in rural areas still wear this style of clothes. They also wear conical straw hats in the sun. The people in large cities prefer styles similar to those in the United States.

(Above) Kite flying has been a very popular pastime for 3,000 years. The kite was probably invented in China.

(Right) Both Chinese children and adults love to play games for fun. One popular game is called mah-jongg. Another name for it is Chinese chess. It is a game similar to chess. The pieces have names such as emperor, knight, and castle. The winner is the first player who gains sets with the highest scores.

Sports and Leisure

Chinese people work very hard and don't have much spare time or money for leisure activities. However, we think it is very important to keep fit. Everyone does exercises before they go to school or work. Many people do slow, gentle exercises called tai chi or a more strenuous martial art, such as kung fu. At school, we play games such as badminton, basketball, table tennis, and volleyball. Recently, Chinese athletes have won many medals at the Olympics. Favorite activities include playing Chinese checkers, flying kites (left), and watching Chinese operas.

The government controls the newspapers, radio, and television. The most widely read newspaper is *The People's Daily*, the official paper of the Communist Party. You can read free newspapers in parks and squares. There are now many television sets in China, and we also listen to the radio. Important official announcements are made by loudspeaker in the parks.

The Peking Opera Troupe is famous throughout the world for its colorful displays combining singing, drama, and acrobatics (right). Chinese Opera has a long history. Today Communist themes are as likely to provide the story line as ancient legends.

Why I'm Here

Under Chairman Mao, people had very little freedom or choice in their lives. During the Cultural Revolution, millions suffered. As a result, many people left China. When Mao died in 1976, the new rulers tried to be more reasonable and allow more freedom. Yet people today are still expected to follow Communist teachings without question.

In 1989, over 100,000 students gathered in Tiananmen Square (meaning Heavenly Peace Gate) in Beijing to demonstrate. They demanded a more democratic government, one without corruption.

They wanted everybody to have a say. The government sent in troops to break up the demonstrations. Thousands of protesters were killed, injured, or arrested. My parents had to leave China, because they supported the students. That is why we came to this country.

The Monument to the People's Heroes overlooks Tiananmen Square in Beijing, the scene of the demonstrations in 1989.

My Future

Since the terrible massacre in Tiananmen Square, the Chinese government has tried to create trade and tourist links with other countries. Now things are gradually changing. The Communist governments in many other places (such as Russia) have been replaced. In China, however, the same leaders that sent troops to break up the demonstrations remain in power. Perhaps one day China will have a less ruthless government, and we will be able to go back. Until then, I will enjoy living in my new home in the West. At first, I found life here difficult. It is so different from life in China. I am glad that we have more freedom here. I can express my ideas and do not get into trouble for speaking out.

(Right) Though parts of China are modernizing rapidly, some things haven't changed very much! There are advantages to living in the West, such as a better standard of living. I hope that one day the people in China will have more freedom, too.

Fact File

Land and People

Official name: People's Republic of China

Language: Putonghua (Mandarin Chinese, the official dialect that originates from Beijing). Other dialects include Yue (Cantonese), Wu, Xiang, Hui, and Hakka.

Population: Over 1.178 billion (estimate mid-1993)

Weather

Climate: China has an enormously varied climate. The south is tropical with an average rainfall of 49–79 inches (125–200 cm) and an average July temperature of 82°F (28°C). By contrast, the north has an average rainfall of less than 30 inches (75 cm) and an average January temperature of -8°F (-22°C).

Cities

Major cities: Beijing (capital), Shanghai, Tianjin, Guangzhou (Canton), Wuhan, Shengyang, Chengdu, and Nanjing

Landmarks

Area: 3,691,521 square miles (9,561,000 sq km)

Major rivers: Chang Jiang (Yangtze), Huang Ho (Yellow)

Highest point: Mt. Everest 29,028 ft. (8,848 m), the highest mountain in the world, lies between Tibet and Nepal.

Culture

Main religions: officially atheist, Confucianism, Buddhism, Taoism

Ethnic groups: Han Chinese (94%), Zhuang, Manchu, Hui, Tibetans, and others

Literacy rate: 70 percent

Food and Farming

Major farm products: Rice, wheat, grains, tea, cotton, silk, tobacco, pigs, chickens, and horses

Government

Form of government: Communist

Trade and Industry

Currency: Yuan

Employment: Agriculture and forestry (60%), service industries (17%), manufacturing industries (18%), construction (5%)

Mineral resources: Coal, natural gas, and limestone

Manufacturing: Clothing and textiles, processed foods, iron and steel, machinery, chemicals

Major exports: Agricultural products, oil, minerals, metals, and manufactured goods (such as clothing and textiles)

Major imports: Grains, chemical fertilizer, steel, industrial raw materials, precision machinery, and luxury goods

Index

Photographic Credits:

Cover, title, pp. 5, 7, 8–9, 14 (top), 19, 20, 22 (top left and bottom), 24 (both), 29: Eye Ubiquitous; cover inset, pp. 3, 14 (bottom), 22 (top right), 28: Roger Vlitos; pp. 4, 13 (right): Andy Burns; p. 10: Hulton Deutsch; pp. 12, 13 (left), 17, 25: John Paul Vlitos; p. 26: Frank Spooner Pictures.